SPORTS BIOGRAPHIES

GEORGE SPRINGER

KENNY ABDO

Fly!
An Imprint of Abdo
abdobooks.com

abdobooks.com

Published by Abdo Zoom, a division of ABDO, P.O. Box 398166, Minneapolis, Minnesota 55439. Copyright © 2019 by Abdo Consulting Group, Inc. International copyrights reserved in all countries. No part of this book may be reproduced in any form without written permission from the publisher. Fly!™ is a trademark and logo of Abdo Zoom.

Printed in the United States of America, North Mankato, Minnesota.
052018
092018

Photo Credits: Alamy, AP Images, Icon Sportswire, iStock
Production Contributors: Kenny Abdo, Jennie Forsberg, Grace Hansen
Design Contributors: Dorothy Toth, Neil Klinepier

Library of Congress Control Number: 2017960656

Publisher's Cataloging-in-Publication Data

Names: Abdo, Kenny, author.
Title: George Springer / by Kenny Abdo.
Description: Minneapolis, Minnesota : Abdo Zoom, 2019. | Series: Sports biographies |
    Includes online resources and index.
Identifiers: ISBN 9781532124785 (lib.bdg.) | ISBN 9781532124921 (ebook) |
    ISBN 9781532124990 (Read-to-me ebook)
Subjects: LCSH: Springer, George--1989-, Biography--Juvenile literature. |
    Baseball players--United States--Biography--Juvenile literature. |
    Outfielders (Baseball)--Biography--Juvenile literature. |
    Houston Astros (Baseball team)--Biography--Juvenile literature.
Classification: DDC 796.35709 [B]--dc23

TABLE OF CONTENTS

GEORGE SPRINGER

George Springer has loved baseball ever since he was a kid. Now, he plays outfield for the Houston Astros.

He was named the **World Series** Most Valuable Player (MVP) in 2017.

EARLY YEARS

Springer was born in New Britain, Connecticut, in 1989. He had a **stutter** from a very young age. He worked hard to overcome it.

Vermont

New Hampshire

New York

Massachusetts

NEW BRITAIN

Rhode Island

Connecticut

Pennsylvania

New Jersey

He was always passionate about sports. He played on the **varsity** baseball team, even as a high school freshman.

At the age of 19, Springer was selected by the Minnesota Twins in the 2008 MLB **draft** while in college. Springer did not feel ready for professional baseball. He did not sign.

GOING PRO

While at the University of Connecticut, Springer was named the Big East Player of the Year. He joined the Houston Astros in 2011.

He made his Major League Baseball (MLB) **debut** in 2014. Springer played right field for his first three seasons. In 2017, he moved to center field.

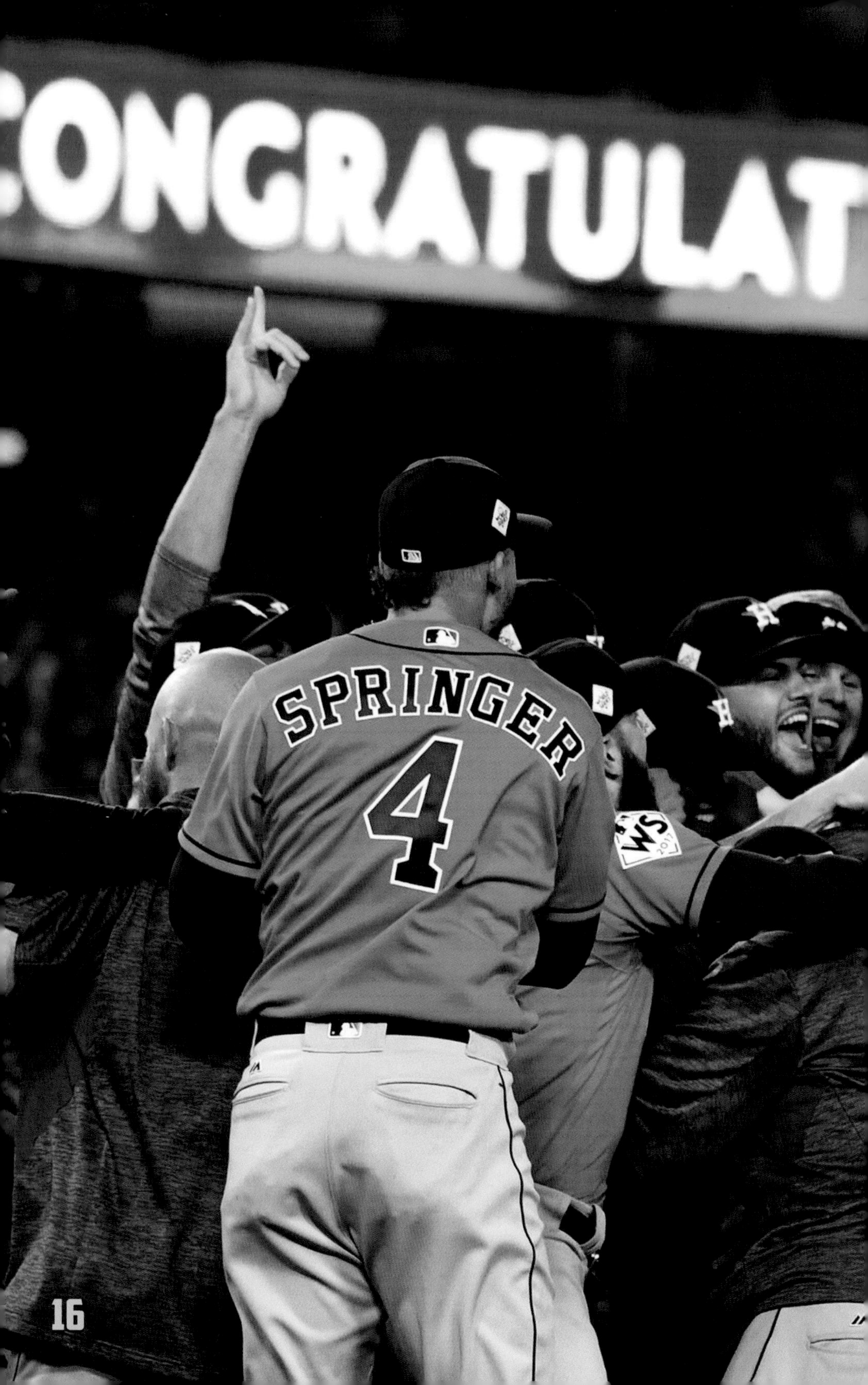
CONGRATULAT
SPRINGER
4
WS
2017

In 2017, the Houston Astros beat the Los Angeles Dodgers in Game 7 of the **World Series**. After, Springer was named MLB All-Star. The World Series champ also received the Silver Slugger award.

Springer set a record by hitting a home run in each of the final four games of the **World Series**. He set another record by getting eight extra base hits.

LEGACY

Springer is a very active **volunteer**. He holds baseball clinics for elementary school students. He is also a **spokesperson** for the Stuttering Association for the Young Foundation in Houston.

GLOSSARY

debut – a first appearance.

draft – a process in sports to assign athletes to a certain team.

spokesperson – a person who speaks on behalf of a group.

stutter – speaking with unintentional repetition of sounds.

varsity – the main team representing a high school in a sports competition.

volunteer – to offer to give one's time to help others without being paid.

World Series – a yearly series of games, where the team who wins a best-of-seven playoff is determined the champions of the year.

ONLINE RESOURCES

Booklinks
NONFICTION NETWORK
FREE! ONLINE NONFICTION RESOURCES

To learn more about George Springer, please visit **abdobooklinks.com**. These links are routinely monitored and updated to provide the most current information available.

INDEX